"protect Your Ideas." A Handbook Of The Laws And Rules Of Practice Relative To Patents, Trade-marks, Copy-rights, Labels, Etc

Stevens, Milo B., & co. [from old catalog]

Nabu Public Domain Reprints:

You are holding a reproduction of an original work published before 1923 that is in the public domain in the United States of America, and possibly other countries. You may freely copy and distribute this work as no entity (individual or corporate) has a copyright on the body of the work. This book may contain prior copyright references, and library stamps (as most of these works were scanned from library copies). These have been scanned and retained as part of the historical artifact.

This book may have occasional imperfections such as missing or blurred pages, poor pictures, errant marks, etc. that were either part of the original artifact, or were introduced by the scanning process. We believe this work is culturally important, and despite the imperfections, have elected to bring it back into print as part of our continuing commitment to the preservation of printed works worldwide. We appreciate your understanding of the imperfections in the preservation process, and hope you enjoy this valuable book.

UNITED STATES PATENT OFFICE

"Protect Your Ideas."

A Hand-book of the Laws and Rules of Practice Relative to Patents, Trade-Marks, Copyrights, Labels, etc.

PREPARED AND PUBLISHED BY

MILO B. STEVENS & CO.,

ATTORNEYS AND SOLICITORS IN PATENT CAUSES.

WASHINGTON, CHICAGO, CLEVELAND,

DETROIT.

Copyright 1908.

INDEX OF SUBJECTS.

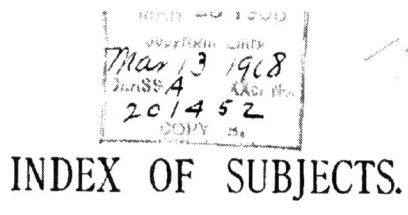

	PAGE
New Inventions	3
The First Step	4
Preliminary Examination of the Patent Office Records	4
Our Fees	6
Sale or Manufacture of Inventions	9
Sale of Patents	9
Rules of Practice of U. S. Patent Office	9
Correspondence	10
Attorneys	10
Inventors' Privilege	11
What May Be Patented	12
Design Patents	13
Caveats	14
Government Fees	15
Models, etc.	16
The Drawings	16
Specimens	17
Secrecy in Patent Office	17
Issue	17
Reissue of Patent	17
Extension of Patent	18
Interferences	18
Renewal of Abandoned Application	18
Renewal of Forfeited Applications	19
Rejected Cases	19
Appeals	20
Foreign Patents	21
Assignments	21
Patent or Trade-Mark. How Soon Secured	22
Deceased or Insane Inventors	22
Porto Rico, Guam and the Philippines	23
Trade-Marks	23
Labels and Prints	26
Copyrights	27
Not Subject to Copyright	27
Fee Contract	29
Testimonials	30

PROTECT YOUR IDEAS.

Have you thought out some improvement in tools or machines you are in the habit of using, or in other articles in daily use? Perhaps you have thought of some labor-saving device, some new process of value, or have conceived a new design in architecture, ornaments or ornamental work, textile fabrics, wall papers, pottery, silverware, cast articles such as type, stoves, etc. You may have a compound or composition, or other goods, wares, or merchandise, that you should not market without a distinctive trade-mark. You may have a musical composition, book, chart, map, dramatic work, engraving, cut, print, drawing, photograph, painting, etc., the copyright of which should be preserved to yourself.

If so, what have you done to **protect your idea,** and secure the pecuniary benefit derivable therefrom?

NEW INVENTIONS.

The official reports of the Commissioner of Patents show that the Patent Office is rapidly approaching the million mark in number of patents granted since the establishment of the office. That there is constant room for improvements in the line of invention is evidenced by the fact that there have been over 20,000 patents granted yearly since 1883. This is the age of invention, and each year sees more new and valuable devices for the home, the shop and the office; improved machinery and processes, time-savers, labor-savers, and conveniences coming on the market; for the most part the product of the inventive genius of the American citizen. All classes of manufacture and trade are on the sharp lookout for something better in their particular lines, and there is an ever-increasing sale for novelties of all sorts.

Small, simple inventions often prove more profitable than more complicated and elaborate productions; the former, being profitably manufactured and sold at a low price, find a readier sale, especially when first introduced, and come into more general use. The metal paper-fasteners, the rubber pencil-tip, the metallic shoe-tip, the metal heel-plate for shoes, the arm-pit dress shield, the wooden shoe-peg, the roller-skate, the return ball, "pigs in clover" puzzle, the "13, 15, 14" puzzle, the "see that hump" hook-and-eye, and numerous other inventions of a comparatively trifling nature, including many toys, games, and the like, have proved very profitable indeed to the patentees. Toys and games, especially those inexpensive in price, usually find a ready market, and in the field of designs or patterns for fabrics, etc., there are many opportunities for profitable invention.

Nearly 25,000 assignments of patent rights are recorded in the Patent Office yearly. This shows an extensive demand for and sale of patented inventions. The number of assignments recorded almost equals the number of patents issued.

We solicit correspondence from inventors on any subject as to which specific information is desired. It is often unsafe to apply general rules to specific cases, and this booklet is not intended to discourage specific inquiry by letter to us.

No Charge whatever will be made for consultation upon any point relative to matters of law and official practice, not involving preparation of papers, search of official records, or consultation of authorities.

THE FIRST STEP.

The first step is to send us **rough pencil sketches** showing all the features of the invention.

A clear description of the invention should accompany the sketch, explaining the several parts or features, their operation and advantages. Refer to the several parts by the use of letters or figures corresponding to like letters or figures on the sketch.

A model or sample need not be sent unless we request it, or unless the inventor finds it easier to explain from the model or sample than from any sketch he can make. If you send a model, see that your name and address are securely attached thereto.

A photograph or series of photographs of a model or sample will often serve as well as the thing itself. Photographs should not be mounted.

No money need be sent as fee for our opinion as to the probable patentability of your invention unless you wish us to make a search of the official records, and whatever information you give us with reference to your invention will be held in strict confidence.

Upon receipt of the description or model of your invention we will inform you whether the invention is of patentable nature, and will give our opinion as to whether a preliminary examination of the official records of U. S. patents is advisable.

PRELIMINARY EXAMINATION OF THE PATENT OFFICE RECORDS.

The objects of the preliminary examination of the official records of prior patents issued by the U. S. Patent Office are:—

1st. To ascertain, **in advance**, as definitely as possible what the probable chances are of securing a patent.

2d. To save the applicant possible useless expenditure of Government fees required to be filed with the application and not recoverable in the event of rejection.

3d. In cases in which contingent terms are desired, to save our clients the attorney's fees for presentation and prosecution of the application, inasmuch as we cannot under any circumstances undertake a case with our fee in the least dependent on a successful outcome, unless a careful search is first made of the official records as above.

The inventor is commonly not justified in filing his application without such preliminary search of the records of prior inventions. An inventor may consider that he is informed as to all patents in the line of his invention, but it is sometimes found that an obscure patent that has not been exploited properly and so is not generally known, stands in the way, and needs to be avoided.

We will purchase and furnish you with **official copies** of patents which possibly conflict with your invention at some point, together with our opinion as to your probable chances of success in seeking protection for yourself.

Our professional opinion, if favorable, should enable you to financially interest others in the matter, if you desire further capital; and you can hardly expect to interest capital, if you wish to do so, unless you can show evidence of a **reasonable prospect** of securing a patent.

The cost of the search is ordinarily but $5.00 attorney's fees, and we credit the amount on the usual charge for our services in prosecuting an application for patent.

We charge this fee in advance in the interest of the legitimate inventor, because of those persons who have not sufficient interest or confidence in their alleged invention or its value, to invest any amount in ascertaining the probable chances of securing a patent, but who would avail themselves of an offer to render this valuable service free of charge, without having, however, any real intention of employing us to secure a patent for them. Properly done, the work of searching the records is no perfunctory task, and it is highly important to the inventor that, if done at all, it be properly done. An attorney who is over-run with curiosity inquirers and triflers, which is apt to be an unavoidable consequence of the "free-search" plan, is naturally unable to give in many instances that due attention and consideration to the matter in hand that the inventor who means business is entitled to and should have.

The preliminary examination or search is among the most important services a patent attorney is called on to perform, i. e., considered from the point of view of his client's interest. In the Patent Office, all U. S. patents heretofore granted are arranged according to the classes and sub-classes, hence patents of all inventions of the same character will, as a rule, be found together, and thousands of patents are sometimes contained in a single class. To make a careful and exhaustive search through the class, or classes, in which an invention may be found, is an operation of exceeding importance to the inventor and often of great difficulty to the attorney.

It is of importance to the inventor in saving a useless expenditure of money in endeavoring to obtain a patent when none can be obtained. Our searches are thorough and complete, and we advise no one to apply unless a good chance of success appears.

Searches made through the Official Gazette, or elsewhere than in Washington, are apt to be incomplete and unreliable. All searches are made by our Washington office, including those ordered by our branch offices at Chicago, Cleveland and Detroit.

If, after such preliminary examination of the records, we are of the opinion that there is a good chance to secure our client a patent, we are willing, if desired, to prosecute the case without further payment of fee if the application is thereafter rejected on any patent issued prior to the filing of the application. We stake our fee on the correctness of our judgment and the care and thoroughness of our preliminary search of the official records of U. S. patents.

If, after preliminary examination, our client feels satisfied, from our report, that his invention is patentably new and wishes to save something on our fee, he can discount it by making a payment of cash in advance, assuming the risk of success himself. Inasmuch as our searches are carefully made, many of our clients prefer to pay cash and make a saving in the cost of the patent.

In any case which we regard as not presenting patentable subject matter, or as being evidently anticipated by prior patents, or as being for any other reason very doubtful, but our client nevertheless wishes to try the case, we invariably require at least part of our fee paid in advance.

OUR FEES.

On a cash basis, in a simple mechanical patent case, not complicated as to the character of the invention, and not becoming involved in interference proceedings, and not requiring an appeal, our entire charge is $30, which includes the fee for the search and for one sheet of drawings.

The manner of payment of this fee is as follows: In the beginning, before the search (see "PRELIMINARY EXAMINATION," page 4), $5. If it appear that the invention is not patentably new, we will so inform the inventor, and he will be to no further expense. But if it appear that the invention has patentable novelty, $15 of our fee and $5 for the drawings, if but one sheet is required, are then payable. On receipt of said amounts we prepare the specification, etc., and send same to the inventor for his approval and signature. When executed, they are to be returned to us together with $5, the balance of our fee, and $15, the Government filing fee. This covers all expenses in a simple case, until the patent is allowed, when the final Government fee of $20 may be paid at any time within six months thereafter. The total cost under this plan is thus $65.

On a contingent basis our total fee in a simple case is $10 greater, or $40, and the manner of payment is as follows: In advance, the $5 fee before the search, as above indicated. If a good chance to secure a patent appear, we will so report to the inventor and send for the Government filing fee of $15, and $5 for the drawings, if but one sheet is required, on receipt of which we will prepare the specification, etc., and send the same to the inventor for approval and signature, and also send him a form of contract for $30 (see page 28) to be signed by himself and a responsible guarantor and returned to us, and on the return thereof we will file the application in the Patent Office, together with the Government filing fee. Thus an application can be put on file for $25, and the remainder of the fees does not have to be paid until the application is allowed and the patent assured.

Payment of our fees in patent and trade-mark cases under the contingent plan is expected upon the termination of the service by the allowance of the application or otherwise according to the terms of our agreement.

Without a search our total fee in a simple case is $25, including one sheet of drawings. If the inventor, by reason of familiarity with the art, or confidence in the novelty of his invention, wishes to apply without an examination, we will undertake a simple case for this very low fee, including one sheet of drawings. In this case we cannot make our fee contingent on success, nor assume responsibility in case the invention is found to be old. Our fee is payable $15 in advance and $10 with return of application for filing.

In complicated cases, which usually require additional sheets of drawings, an extra charge will be made according to the nature and amount of additional or extraordinary work involved. This charge will be moderate and reasonable, and the applicant will be informed thereof when the report on the search is made, in advance of the preparation of the case.

In design patent cases our charge is ordinarily $25, including the cost of the usual one sheet of drawings. If not paid in advance, the entire charge as above is $10 more. The amount of professional work is the same and the fee the same, irrespective of the term for which the design patent is issued, the saving to the claimant being in the smaller Government fee for the shorter term.

For preparing and filing a caveat, our entire charge will ordinarily be $20, including the cost of the usual one sheet of drawings. This amount will be payable strictly in advance of the preparing of the papers, and will be entirely independent of the fee for preparing and prosecuting the application for patent, and will not be considered as part fee on account of any interference proceedings which may arise.

For renewing a caveat our fee will ordinarily be $5, payable in advance.

In a reissue of patent case our fee is ordinarily the same as in an original application.

In a matter of trade-mark registration our entire charge is ordinarily $12.50 or less (including drawings), according to the nature of the case.

If not paid in advance the entire charge is $2.50 more.

In a matter of label or print registration our entire charge is ordinarily $10, payable in advance.

In a matter of copyright our entire charge is ordinarily $6, including the Government fee, and is payable in advance.

For each sheet of official drawings required by the Patent Office in patent, design patent and trade-mark cases our charge is $5. Ordinarily but one sheet is required in a case.

Rejected, abandoned, neglected and forfeited cases, appeals, interference and infringement cases, and all other forms of patent litigation, in the Patent Office or United States Courts, will be conducted on moderate terms, mutually agreed upon.

If an inventor has applied for a patent, either with or without an attorney, and the application has been rejected or is not receiving satisfactory attention, we can undertake the matter and may be able to secure an allowance. In any such case the inventor should give us a statement of the facts, on receipt of which we will send a power of attorney. Our fee in such cases will depend on the amount of work necessary to be done, but will ordinarily be considerably less than the fee in an original case.

For preparing and filing assignments our fee is $5 or more, according to the character of the assignment; our charge to include the Government fee, which is from $1 to $3, according to the amount of matter.

For making an abstract of title of a patent or trade-mark, being a digest of recorded assignments filed in a case, our fee will ordinarily be $5, including the Government fees.

Official printed copies of drawings and specifications of patents will be furnished at 10 cents each

Manuscript copies of record and blue-prints of drawings not printed, will be furnished at reasonable rates according to amount of matter and dimensions of drawings.

Foreign patents: Our fees in foreign patent cases will be stated on application.

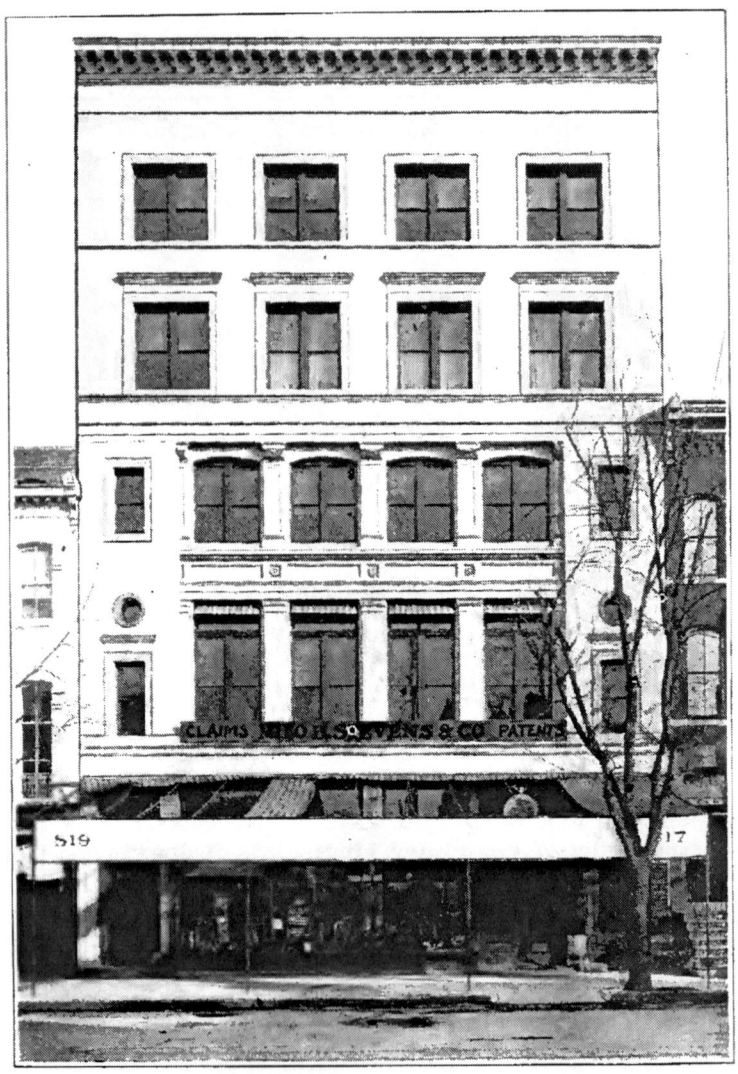

THE POPE BUILDING, 817-819 14TH STREET

SALE OR MANUFACTURE OF INVENTIONS.

An inventor lacking the means to obtain a patent can in most cases obtain the money necessary by assigning an interest in the invention, or an exclusive right in part of the United States, to the person furnishing the money. Such a person is to be looked for among the inventor's friends, or among manufacturers of the class of goods to which the invention pertains. A favorable report as to patentable novelty (see "Preliminary Examination," page 4) may be of great assistance in inducing some person to furnish the capital.

We do not prosecute cases for an interest in the patent, since we are not in a position to make practical use of inventions. Offers to this end must be uniformly declined.

A list of manufacturers interested in the particular line or class to which the invention belongs, will, if desired, be furnished free to all applicants who apply through us, or whose patents are secured through our agency.

We will advertise for sale, free of charge, in **The National Tribune**, the great Washington weekly (one insertion), any patent secured through our agency, if desired. The Tribune has a national circulation of nearly 100,000 per week.

SALE OF PATENTS.

Manufacturers and others are vitally interested in securing by purchase patents for meritorious inventions. The success of their industries depends upon their keeping abreast of the times, and as a rule an enterprising manufacturer desires to keep ahead of his competitors by adopting new methods or processes, or by producing new articles of manufacture. The annual reports of the Commissioner of Patents show a constantly increasing number of patents issued. It is safe to say that over 20,000 patents are sold yearly by the inventors, and the indications are that there is a good and increasing market for meritorious inventions of all kinds, even though they mark but a slight improvement in the arts to which they relate.

We will aid our clients who desire to sell their patents, or rights thereunder, to bring their inventions directly to the attention of manufacturers and others who may be interested.

RULES OF PRACTICE OF U. S. PATENT OFFICE.

The rules of practice of the Patent Office are based upon the statutory law governing the granting of patents, and set out very fully the official requirements with respect to the transaction of business before the Patent Office. In the matter following the rules are freely quoted as being the best evidence of what is necessary to do or to avoid doing in any matter coming within the purview of the Commissioner of Patents.

CORRESPONDENCE.

Rule 1. "All business with the office should be transacted in writing. Unless by the consent of all parties, the action of the office will be based exclusively on the written record. No attention will be paid to any alleged oral promise, stipulation, or understanding in relation to which there is a disagreement or doubt."

Rule 4. "**The personal attendance of applicants at the Patent Office is unnecessary.** Their business can be transacted by correspondence."

Rule 5. "The assignee of the entire interest of an invention is entitled to hold correspondence with the office to the exclusion of the inventor."

Rule 7. "When an attorney shall have filed his power of attorney, duly executed, the correspondence will be held with him."

Rule 8. "A double correspondence with the inventor and an assignee, or with a principal and his attorney, or with two attorneys, can not generally be allowed."

The following extracts from the official rules of practice in the U. S. Patent Office contain matters not included in the foregoing and may be of information and interest to inventors:

ATTORNEYS.

Rule 14. "The Office **can not respond to inquiries as to the novelty** of an alleged invention in advance of the filing of an application for a patent, **nor to inquiries propounded with a view to ascertaining whether any alleged improvements have been patented**, and, if so, to whom; nor can it act as an expounder of the patent law, nor as counsellor for individuals, except as to questions arising within the office.

"Of the propriety of making an application for a patent, the inventor must judge for himself. The office is open to him, and its records and models pertaining to all patents granted may be inspected either by himself or by any attorney or expert he may call to his aid, and its reports are widely distributed. Further than this the office can render him no assistance until his case comes regularly before it in the manner prescribed by law." (Rev. Stat., Secs. 475, 481, 484, 4883.)

Rule 17. "**An applicant or an assignee of the entire interest** may prosecute his own case, but he **is advised, unless familiar with such matters, to employ a competent attorney**, as the value of patents depends largely upon the skillful preparation of the specification and claims. The office can not aid in the selection of an attorney."

Rule 23. "Inasmuch as **applications can not be examined out of their regular order,** except in accordance with the provisions of Rule 63, and **members of Congress can neither examine nor act in patent cases without written powers of attorney,** applicants are advised not to impose upon Senators or Representatives labor which will consume their time without any advantageous results."

The true value of a patent depends upon the manner in which the claims are drawn and worded. Many patents are so drawn by incompetent persons, or persons who are not legally capable of drawing claims, that the patent affords little, if any, protection to the inventor, in fact, often losing to the inventor the protection to which he is entitled. It is as necessary to have a patent carefully drawn as it is to have properly drawn the deed to a piece of property, so that if your invention is new, the claim will not only cover what you have made but various modifications and changes in form. A patent covers only what is claimed. The proper wording of the claims is a work of extreme difficulty, and no inventor is justified in placing his case in the hands of any person not having the requisite legal and technical skill. Walker, in his Treatise on Patents, says:

"Writing a claim for a patent may require as many points of information and powers of mind as can ever be required for any prose writing of similar length. More than half the chapters of this book contain such points of information, but neither this nor any other law book can embody all that the penner of such a claim requires to know."

Washington attorneys are usually best situated to serve the interests of inventors to the fullest advantage Most attorneys at a distance from the Capital rely upon Washington correspondents or associates for important portions of the work of preparing and conducting the case.

Our Western branches, at Chicago, Cleveland and Detroit, will afford many having business before the Patent Office the advantage of conferring in person with our representatives who will attend to the matter through the main office at Washington.

We are convinced that an attorney having a Washington office is prepared for better service than one not having the same, or than one who works through an associate here. This is one of the reasons why we maintain our Washington office And with respect to clients within reach of our Western offices, we have the combined advantage of an office here for work before the Office and a local office for personal consultation.

INVENTORS' PRIVILEGE.

The official weekly list of patents issued may be inspected personally, without charge, by inventors calling at any of our offices. The principal features of the drawings and most important claims of each patent are shown.

WHAT MAY BE PATENTED.

Patents are obtainable under section 4886 Revised Statutes, which as amended by the act of March 3, 1897, taking effect January 1, 1898, provides,

"Any person who has invented or discovered any new and useful art, machine. manufacture, or composition of matter, or any new and useful improvements thereof, not known or used by others in this country **before his invention or discovery thereof,** and not patented or described in any printed publication in this or any foreign country before his invention or discovery thereof, **or more than two years prior to his application,** and not in public use or on sale in this country for more than two years prior to his application, unless the same is proved to have been abandoned, may, upon payment of the fees required by law and other due proceedings had, obtain a patent therefor."

The term of a patent: "Every patent shall contain * * * a grant to the patentee, his heirs or assigns, for the term of **seventeen years,** of the exclusive right to make, use and vend the invention throughout the United States and the Territories thereof, referring to the specification for the particulars thereof. A copy of the specification and drawing shall be annexed to the patent and be a part thereof." Rev. Stat., Sec. 4884.

Conceiving the idea of an improvement or new device, etc., is of no avail unless the scheme is reduced to tangible form by model, sketch, draft, or otherwise in advance of another person conceiving the same or a similar idea. Nor can an inventor safely allow his invention to lie in an incomplete state; he must use all due diligence to complete and perfect his invention.

A prior similar device of another person, temporarily in use, would not be regarded as an anticipatory invention if it is shown to have been abandoned under circumstances indicating that it was no more than an abortive and unsuccessful experiment.

Experimental use of an invention, either by the inventor or others at his request, with a view to testing and perfecting the device or improvement, does not impair the rights of the inventor to a patent. More than this before application for patent may be construed as a donation of the invention to the public and a patent refused. If after completion an invention becomes a successful experiment, yet the invention does not pass absolutely from the domain of experiment until it has been actually used in public. If abandoned **before** such public use, it is an abandoned experiment and may be patented by a subsequent inventor If abandoned **after** such public use, it becomes the property of the public and cannot be patented. **If forgotten** either before or after such public use, it may be reinvented and patented by a subsequent inventor.

A change of an old device is patentable, even though simple, if it is effective in producing a new and useful result.

A novel combination of old devices or instrumentalities, producing a new and useful result, is a patentable invention.

All uses and advantages belonging to an invention fall to the inventor, even though he failed to perceive or state advantages discovered by others; for the discovery of a new use for an old machine is not patentable.

Mere substitution of a material or of a mechanical equivalent is not patentable, unless the result is an improvement.

The term "useful" in the patent law is to be understood as in contradistinction to **mischievous**.

A principle, function, or abstract effect cannot be patented.

Separate patents must be procured for separate inventions.

Rule 41. "Two or more independent inventions cannot be claimed in one application; but where several distinct inventions are dependent upon each other and mutually contribute to produce a single result they may be claimed in one application.

This rule should be remembered by inventors. Division of an application held to cover more than one invention, or restriction to a single invention is frequently required by the Patent Office before the application will be considered. It is therefore often necessary to file several applications to cover the whole invention, where it consists of several parts any one of which may be used independently.

Knowledge or use in foreign countries: Rule 27. "If it appear that the inventor, at the time of making his application, believed himself to be the first inventor or discoverer, a patent will not be refused on account of the invention or discovery, or any part thereof, having been known or used in any foreign country before his invention or discovery thereof, if it had not been before patented or described in any printed publication." (Rev. Stat., Sec. 4887.)

DESIGN PATENTS.

Design Patents are obtainable under section 4929, Revised Statutes, as amended by Act of May 9, 1902, which provides:

"Any person who has invented any new, original and ornamental design for an article of manufacture, not known or used by others in this country before his invention thereof and not patented or described in any printed publication in this or any foreign country before his invention thereof, or more than two years prior to his application, and not in public use or on sale in this country for more than two years prior to his application, unless the same is proved to have been abandoned, may, upon payment of the fees required by law and other due proceedings had, the same as in cases of inventions or discoveries covered by section forty-eight hundred and eighty-six, obtain a patent therefor."

The object of design patents is the encouragement of the arts of decoration rather than the invention of useful products; but by section 4933, Revised Statutes, all the regulations and provisions which apply to obtaining or protecting patents for inventions or discoveries are made applicable to design patents so far as consistent therewith.

A design patent will cover not only the exact form or configuration prescribed by the patent, but also those which have so close a resemblance as to seem identical to the ordinary observer. The owner of a design patent may not be defrauded of his rights by an unscrupulous imitation varying from the genuine only in some immaterial points.

The term of design patents is three and one-half years, seven years, or fourteen years, as the applicant may, in his application, elect. (Rev Stat, Sec. 4931)

Having elected, he cannot change or extend the term.

CAVEATS.

Rule 183. "A caveat, under the patent law, is a notice given to the Patent Office of the caveator's claim as inventor, in order to prevent the grant of a patent to another person for the same alleged invention upon an application filed during the life of the caveat without notice to the caveator."

Rule 184. "Any citizen of the United States who has made a new invention or discovery and desires further time to mature the same may, on payment of a fee of ten dollars, file in the Patent Office a caveat setting forth the object and the distinguishing characteristics of the invention, and praying protection of his right until he shall have matured his invention. Such caveat shall be filed in the confidential archives of the office and preserved in secrecy and shall be operative for the term of one year from the filing thereof." (Rev. Stat., Sec. 4902.)

Rule 185. "The caveat may be renewed, on request in writing, by the payment of a second caveat fee of ten dollars, and it will continue in force for one year from the date of the payment of such second fee. Subsequent renewals may be made with like effect. If a caveat be not renewed, it will still be preserved in the secret archives of the office."

Rule 186. "An alien has the same privilege, if he has resided in the United States one year next preceding the filing of his caveat, and has made oath of his intention to become a citizen." (Rev. Stat, Sec. 4902)

Rule 191. "If at any time within one year after the filing or renewal of a caveat another person shall file an application for an invention which would in any manner interfere with the invention set forth in such caveat, then such application will be suspended and notice thereof will be sent to the person filing the caveat. (Rev. Stat., Sec. 4902.)

"If the caveator shall file a complete application within the time prescribed, and if the invention be found patentable, he will be entitled to an interference with the previous application, for the purpose of proving priority of invention and obtaining the patent if he be adjudged the prior inventor. The caveator, if he would avail himself of his caveat, must file his application within three months from the expiration of the time regularly required for the transmission to him of the notice deposited in the post office at Washington. The day on which the time for filing expires will be mentioned in the notice or indorsement thereon."

Rule 192. "The caveator will not be entitled to notice of any application pending at the time of filing his caveat, nor of any application filed after the expiration of one year from the date of the filing or renewal thereof."

Rule 193. "A caveat confers no rights and affords no protection except as to notice of an interfering application filed during its life, giving the caveator the opportunity of proving priority of invention if he so desires. It may be used as evidence in contests, as provided in Rule 154."

Rule 194. "There is no provision of law making the caveat assignable, although the alleged invention therein set forth is assignable, and the caveat may be used as means of identifying the invention transferred in an assignment."

GOVERNMENT FEES.

Rule 203. "Nearly all the fees payable to the Patent Office are positively required by law to be paid in advance—that is, upon making application for any action by the office for which a fee is payable. For the sake of uniformity and convenience the remaining fees will be required to be paid in the same manner." (Rev. Stat., Sec. 4893.)

On filing each original or new application for patent (except design patent)	$15
On allowance of each original or new application for patent (except design patent)	20
On filing each original or new application for design patent, for 3½ years	10
On filing each original or new application for design patent, for seven years	15
On filing each original or new application for design patent, for 14 years	30
On filing or renewing a caveat	10
On filing an application for reissue of a patent	30
On filing an appeal to the Board of Examiners-in-Chief	10
On filing an appeal to the Commissioner in person	20

On filing an application for registration or renewal of a trade-mark.... $10
On filing an application for registration of a label or print.......... 6
On filing an application for copyright 1
On recording an assignment, from $1 to $3.

MODELS, ETC.

Rule 56. "A model will only be required or admitted as a part of the application when on examination of the case in its regular order the primary examiner shall find it to be necessary or useful. In such case, if a model has not been furnished, the examiner shall notify the applicant of such requirement, which will constitute an official action in the case."

Models of designs are not required when the design can be sufficiently represented by a drawing

A rough model of an invention for our information in making the search and preparing the case, will often be found useful, and if the inventor have a model it should be sent to us, preferably when the search is ordered. But if the invention can be shown by rough drawings and a written explanation, a model need not be made nor sent. The material of which a model for our information is made is of no importance, the only purpose being to convey the idea.

The inventor's name and address should be securely pasted or otherwise securely fixed to the model, whether sent for the information of the Patent Office or for the attorney alone.

THE DRAWINGS.

Rule 49. "The applicant for a patent is required by law to furnish a drawing of his invention whenever the nature of the case admits of it." (Rev. Stat, Sec. 4889.)

Rule 55. "Applicants are advised to employ competent artists to make their drawings."

The official drawings so required are so defined and restricted by official regulation that only draftsmen thoroughly familiar and skilled in the preparation of Patent Office drawings can be relied on to properly and fully meet the official requirements.

One sheet of drawings is usually required to be filed with each application for patent, design patent, caveat, reissue, renewal of abandoned or rejected application, trade-mark, etc Additional sheets may be required by the nature of the invention to properly illustrate it.

We attend to the preparation of the drawings required in all cases filed through us. Owing to the strict technical requirements as to the drawing, it is necessary to have them made by some one experienced in making drawings for the Patent Office, Otherwise much time and money may be wasted.

SPECIMENS.

Rule 62. "When the invention or discovery is a composition of matter, the applicant, if required by the Commissioner, shall furnish specimens of the composition, and of its ingredients, sufficient in quantity for the purpose of experiment. In all cases where the article is not perishable, a specimen of the composition claimed, put up in proper form to be preserved by the office, must be furnished. (Rules 56, 60 and 61 apply to specimens also.)" (Rev. Stat., Sec. 4890.)

SECRECY IN PATENT OFFICE.

Rule 15. "**Caveats and pending applications are preserved in secrecy.** No information will be given, without authority, respecting the filing by any particular person of a caveat or of an application for a patent or for the reissue of a patent, the pendency of any particular case before the office, or the subject-matter of any particular application, unless it shall be necessary to the proper conduct of business before the office, as provided by Rules 97, 103 and 108," (concerning interferences). (Rev. Stat., Sec. 4902.)

ISSUE.

Rule 164. "If, on examination, it shall appear that the applicant is justly entitled to a patent under the law, a notice of allowance will be sent him or his attorney, calling for the payment of the final fee within six months from the date of such notice of allowance, upon the receipt of which within the time fixed by law the patent will be prepared for issue." (Rev. Stat., Secs. 4885, 4893, 4897.)

Rule 165. "After notice of the allowance of an application is given, the case will not be withdrawn from issue except by approval of the Commissioner, and if withdrawn for further action on the part of the office a new notice of allowance will be given. When the final fee has been paid upon an application for letters patent, and the case has received its date and number, it will not be withdrawn or suspended from issue on account of any mistake or change of purpose of the applicant or his attorney, nor for the purpose of enabling the inventor to procure a foreign patent, nor for any other reasons except mistake on the part of the office, or because of fraud, or illegality in the application, or for interference."

REISSUE OF PATENT.

Rule 85 "A reissue is granted to the original patentee, his legal representatives, or the assignees of the entire interest, when the original patent is inoperative or invalid by reason of a defective or insufficient specification, or by reason of the patentee claiming as his invention or discovery more than he had a right to claim as new, provided the error has arisen through inadvertence, accident, or mistake, and without any fraudulent or deceptive intention. (Rev. Stat., Secs. 4895, 4916.)

"Reissue applications must be made and the specifications sworn to by the inventors, if they be living."

No new matter can be introduced in reissue specifications, and if improvements are to be protected, regular application for patents thereon must be made.

The period of protection under the reissue is not extended beyond the date when the original patent would have expired, the reissue dating from the date of the original issue.

EXTENSION OF PATENT.

The extension of the period of protection of a patent or design patent is possible only by authority of a special act of Congress in the particular case, a discrimination extremely difficult to secure.

The better method of extension is by improvement of the original invention and securing of new patents on the improvements.

INTERFERENCES.

Rule 93. "An interference is a proceeding instituted for the purpose of determining the question of priority of invention between two or more parties claiming substantially the same patentable invention. The fact that one of the parties has already obtained a patent will not prevent an interference, for, although the Commissioner has no power to cancel a patent, he may grant another patent for the same invention to a person who proves to be the prior inventor." (Rev. Stat., Sec. 4904.)

Rule 146. "In interference cases parties have the same remedy by appeal to the examiners-in-chief, to the Commissioner, and to the Court of Appeals of the District of Columbia, as in *ex parte* cases." (Rev. Stat., Secs. 4904, 4909, 4910, 4911.) (Sec. 9, act of Feb. 9, 1893.)

RENEWAL OF ABANDONED APPLICATION.

Rule 77. "If an applicant neglect to prosecute his application for *one year* after the date when the last official notice of any action by the office was mailed to him, the application will be held to be abandoned, as set forth in Rule 171." (Rev. Stat., Sec. 4894.)

Rule 171 "An abandoned application is one which has not been completed and prepared for examination within *one year* after the filing of the petition, or which the applicant has failed to prosecute within *one year* after any action therein of which notice has been duly given, or which the applicant has expressly abandoned by filing in the office a written declaration of abandonment, signed by himself and assignee, if any, identifying his application by title of invention, serial number, and date of filing. (Rev. Stat., Sec. 4894.)

"Prosecution of an application to save it from abandonment must include such proper action as the condition of the case may require. The admission of an amendment not responsive to the last official action, or refusal to admit the same, and any proceedings relative thereto, shall not operate to save the application from abandonment under section 4894 of the Revised Statutes"

Rule 172. "Before an application abandoned by failure to complete or prosecute can be revived as a pending application, it must be shown to the satisfaction of the Commissioner that the delay in the prosecution of the same was unavoidable" (Rev. Stat., Sec 4894.)

Rule 173. "When a new application is filed in place of an abandoned or rejected application, a new specification, oath, drawing, and fee will be required; but the old model, if suitable, may be used."

A new application should be filed if the delay in prosecution is regarded as not unavoidable; provided that the invention has not been in public use or on sale for more than two years.

RENEWAL OF FORFEITED APPLICATION.

Rule 174. "A forfeited application is one upon which a patent has been withheld for failure to pay the final fee within the prescribed time."

Rule 175. "When the patent has been withheld by reason of nonpayment of the final fee, any person, whether inventor or assignee, who has an interest in the invention for which such patent was ordered to issue may file a renewal of the application for the same invention; but such second application must be made within two years after the allowance of the original application. Upon the hearing of such new application abandonment will be considered as a question of fact." (Rev. Stat, Sec 4897.)

Rule 176. "In such renewal the oath, petition, specification, drawing, and model of the original application may be used for the second application, but a new fee will be required. The second application will not be regarded for all purposes as a continuation of the original one, but must bear date from the time of renewal and be subject to examination like an original application."

REJECTED CASES.

Imperfect or incomplete specifications often result in the rejection of applications. Lack of skill in other respects may also result in rejection.

A mere matter of opinion may be the cause of the rejection, as the judgment of the examiners and officers of the Patent Office is not infallible, however skilled.

Further prosecution of the matter may be warranted under any of the above circumstances, by various courses of procedure familiar to practitioners before the Patent Office.

APPEALS.

After rejection by the Primary Examiner, an appeal may be taken to the Board of Examiners-in-Chief.

The Commissioner of Patents in person may be appealed to from the adverse decision of the Board of Examiners-in-Chief.

The Court of Appeals of the District of Columbia considers appeals from the adverse personal decision of the Commissioner of Patents.

Following are Patent Office rules pertaining thereto.

Rule 133. "Every applicant for a patent, any of the claims of whose application have been twice rejected for the same reasons, upon grounds involving the merits of the invention, such as lack of invention, novelty, or utility, or on the ground of abandonment, public use or sale, inoperativeness of invention, aggregation of elements, incomplete combination of elements, or, when amended, for want of identity with the invention originally disclosed, or because the amendment involves a departure from the invention originally presented; and every applicant for the reissue of a patent whose claims have been twice rejected for any of the reasons above enumerated, or on the ground that the original patent is not inoperative or invalid, or if so inoperative or invalid that the errors which rendered it so did not arise from inadvertence, accident, or mistake, may, upon payment of a fee of $10, appeal from the decision of the primary examiner to the examiners-in-chief. The appeal must set forth in writing the points of the decision upon which it is taken, and must be signed by the applicant or his duly authorized attorney or agent " (Rev. Stat., Sec. 4909)

Rule 140. "From the adverse decision of the Board of Examiners-in-Chief appeal may be taken to the Commissioner in person, upon payment of the fee of $20 required by law." (Rev. Stat., Sec. 4910)

Rule. 148. "From the adverse decision of the Commissioner upon the claims of an application and in interference cases, an appeal may be taken to the Court of Appeals of the District of Columbia in the manner prescribed by the rules of that court." (Rev. Stat., Sec. 4911; Sec. 9, act Feb. 9, 1893)

Rule 150. "*Pro forma* proceedings will not be had in the Patent Office for the purpose of securing to applicants an appeal to the Court of Appeals of the District of Columbia."

FOREIGN PATENTS.

Foreign patents should be applied for before the issue of the U. S patent, although in those countries which are members of the International Union a patent may be applied for within one year after the filing of the U. S. application; or in Canada and a few other countries, within one year after the *issue* of the U. S. patent.

The six months allowed by law for payment of final U S. fee, after allowance of application, gives sufficient time for the preparation and filing of foreign applications before the issue of U. S. patent.

The period of protection under foreign patents ranges from seven years, in the Bahama Islands and Barbadoes, to twenty years, in Spain and Belgium, the terms elsewhere being generally fifteen years.

The cost of foreign patents varies considerably and will be stated particularly upon inquiry as to any country or countries.

Effect of foreign patents on U. S. application: The receipt of letters patent from a foreign government will not prevent the inventor from obtaining a patent in the United States, unless the application on which the foreign patent was granted was filed more than twelve months prior to the filing of the application in this country, in which case no patent will be granted in this country. (Rev. Stat., Sec. 4887.)

ASSIGNMENTS.

Rule 196. "Every patent or any interest therein shall be assignable by law by an instrument in writing, and the patentee or his assigns or legal representatives may, in like manner, grant and convey an exclusive right under the patent to the whole or any specified part of the United States" (Rev Stat., Sec. 4898.)

Rule 198. "An assignment, grant, or conveyance of a patent will be void as against any subsequent purchaser or mortgagee for a valuable consideration without notice unless recorded in the Patent Office within three months from the date thereof." (Rev. Stat, Sec. 4898)

Rule 26 "In case of an assignment of the whole interest in the invention, or of the whole interest in the patent to be granted, the patent will, upon request of the applicant embodied in the assignment, issue to the assignee; and if the assignee hold an undivided part interest, the patent will, upon like request, issue jointly to the inventor and the assignee; but the assignment in either case must first have been entered of record, and at a day not later than the date of the payment of the final fee; and if it be dated subsequently to the execution of the application, it must give the date of execution of the application, or the date of filing, or the serial number, so that there can be no mistake as to the particular invention intended. The application and oath must be signed by the actual inventor, if alive, even if the patent is to issue to an assignee; if the inventor be dead, the application may be made by the executor or administrator." (Rev. Stat., Sec. 4895.)

Rule 28. "Joint inventors are entitled to a joint patent; neither of them can obtain a patent for an invention jointly invented by them. Independent inventors of distinct and independent improvements in the same machine can not obtain a joint patent for their separate inventions. The fact that one person furnishes the capital and another makes the invention does not entitle them to make an application as joint inventors; but in such case they may become joint patentees, upon the conditions prescribed in Rule 26."

Licenses and shop-rights, which are not exclusive, need not be recorded.

We prepare and record assignments, licenses, etc.

PATENT OR TRADE-MARK.

How Soon Secured.

Rule 63. "Applications filed in the Patent Office are classified according to the various arts, and are taken up for examination in regular order of filing, those in the same class of invention being examined and disposed of, as far as practicable, in the order in which the respective applications are completed."

The time necessary to secure allowance of a patent or trade-mark application is often very short—from one to four months—but some of the divisions of the Patent Office are so far behind in their work that a longer time is required. We consider time of minor importance as compared to a broad and valid patent. The broader claims naturally meet the most objection in the Patent Office. It is not well to sacrifice broad claims to secure an allowance in a shorter time. As the final Government fee need not be paid till six months after the granting of the patent, the actual issue may be deferred for that period after the right to patent is ascertained.

DECEASED OR INSANE INVENTORS.

Rule 25 "In case of the death of the inventor the application will be made by and the patent will issue to his executor or administrator. In such case the oath required by Rule 46 will be made by the executor or administrator. In case of the death of the inventor during the time intervening between the filing of his application and the granting of a patent thereon, the letters patent will issue to the executor or administrator upon proper intervention by him. (Rev. Stat., Sec. 4896.)

"In case an inventor becomes insane, the application may be made by and the patent issued to his legally appointed guardian, conservator, or representative, who will make the oath required by Rule 46." (Act of February 28, 1899.)

PORTO RICO, GUAM AND THE PHILIPPINES.

The protection of patents, trade-marks, labels and prints, duly issued under United States laws, is by an order of the War Department, dated April 11, 1899, extended to all territory acquired from Spain or under American military control.

Registration is necessary, a proper certificate being required to be filed with the Governor-General of the respective provinces.

Our fee for each certificate is $5, including all Patent Office fees.

TRADE-MARKS.

Registration of trade-marks is provided for by the recent act of February 20, 1905, in force from and after April 1, 1905, and superseding the former laws on the subject. The most important feature of the new act is the providing of effectual protection for trade-marks used in commerce "among the several States"—which includes the territories and all U. S. possessions beyond seas. Under former laws no enforceable protection was provided save for marks actually used in commerce with "foreign nations or Indian tribes."

The main provisions of the new act are substantially as follows:

The owner of any trade-mark used in commerce with foreign nations, or among the several States, or with Indian tribes, may obtain registration by making proper application to the Commissioner of Patents. A foreign applicant must reside or be located in a foreign country which affords similar privileges to citizens of the United States, and must designate some person or agent resident in the United States, on whom process or notice of proceedings affecting the trade-mark may be served.

Registration will be refused if a mark consists of or comprises immoral or scandalous matter; or comprises the flag or coat of arms of the United States, or any simulation thereof, or of any State, municipality, or foreign nation; or the emblem of any fraternal society; or the red cross of the National Red Cross; or is "identical with a registered or known trade-mark owned and in use by another and appropriated to merchandise of the same descriptive qualities, as to be likely to cause confusion or mistake in the mind of the public, or to deceive purchasers;" or consists merely in the name of an individual, firm, or corporation, not written, printed, impressed or woven in some particular or distinctive manner, or in association with a portrait of the individual; or is "descriptive of the goods on which the mark is to be used, or of the character or quality of such goods;" or is "merely a geographical name or term." Also, a portrait of a living person can not be registered except with his consent.

An established trade-mark of any kind can be registered, if in actual and exclusive use as a trade-mark by the applicant or his predecessors for ten years or more previous to February 20, 1905. In other words, all exclusive marks at least ten years old on February 20, 1905, can be registered, notwithstanding they may be subject to some of the objections indicated above. This will permit the registration of many established marks which it has heretofore been impossible to register because they are **descriptive, or geographical,** or otherwise objectionable.

Opposition to registration of any trade-mark; cancellation of such registration; and the determination of interferences involving the question of prior right, whether between different applicants for registration of the same or similar marks, or between an applicant and a prior registrant, are provided for by the new act.

Assignments of trade-marks may be made in connection with the good will of a business. Unless recorded in the Patent Office within three months from date thereof an assignment is void against a subsequent purchaser for value without notice of the prior assignment.

The term of trade-mark registration is twenty years, renewable for a like period as often as desired.

The protection or rights afforded by the registration of trademark are specified in the law as follows:

"Sec. 16. That the registration of a trade-mark under the provisions of this Act shall be prima facie evidence of ownership. Any person who shall, without the consent of the owner thereof, reproduce, counterfeit, copy, or colorably imitate any such trade-mark and affix the same to merchandise of substantially the same descriptive properties as those set forth in the registration, or to labels, signs, prints, packages, wrappers, or receptacles intended to be used upon or in connection with the sale of merchandise of substantially the same descriptive properties as those set forth in such registration, and shall use, or shall have used, such reproduction, counterfeit, copy, or colorable imitation in commerce among the several States, or with a foreign nation, or with the Indian tribes, shall be liable to an action for damages therefor at the suit of the owner thereof; and whenever in any such action a verdict is rendered for the plaintiff, the court may enter judgment therein for any sum above the amount found by the verdict as the actual damages, according to the circumstances of the case, not exceeding three times the amount of such verdict, together with the costs."

*   *   *   *   *   *

"Sec. 19. That the several courts vested with jurisdiction of cases arising under the present Act shall have power to grant injunctions, according to the course and principles of equity, to prevent the violation of

INTERIOR VIEW OF OUR WASHINGTON OFFICE

any right of the owner of a trade-mark registered under this Act, on such terms as the court may deem reasonable; and upon a decree being rendered in any such case for wrongful use of a trade-mark the complainant shall be entitled to recover, in addition to the profits to be accounted for by the defendant, the damages the complainant has sustained thereby, and the court shall assess the same or cause the same to be assessed under its direction. The court shall have the same power to increase such damages, in its discretion, as is given by section sixteen of this Act for increasing damages found by verdict in actions of law; and in assessing profits the plaintiff shall be required to prove the defendant's sales only; defendant must prove all elements of cost which are claimed."

"Sec. 20. That in any case involving the right to a trade-mark registered in accordance with the provisions of this Act, in which the verdict has been found for the plaintiff, or an injunction issued, the court may order that all labels, signs, prints, packages, wrappers, or receptacles in the posession of the defendant, bearing the trade-mark of the plaintiff or complainant, or any reproduction, counterfeit, copy, or colorable imitation thereof, shall be delivered up and destroyed. Any injunction that may be granted upon hearing, after notice to the defendant, to prevent the violation of any right of the owner of a trade-mark registered in accordance with the provisions of this Act, by any circuit court of the United States, or by a judge thereof, may be served on the parties against whom such injunction may be granted anywhere in the United States where they may be found, and shall be operative, and may be enforced by proceedings to punish for contempt, or otherwise by the court by which such injunction was granted, or by any other circuit court, or judge thereof, in the United States, or by the supreme court of the District of Columbia, or a judge thereof. The said courts, or judges thereof, shall have jurisdiction to enforce said injunction, as herein provided, as fully as if the injunction had been granted by the circuit court in which it is sought to be enforced. The clerk of the court or judge granting the injunction shall, when required to do so by the court before which application to enforce said injunction is made, transfer without delay to said court a certified copy of all the papers on which the said injunction was granted that are on file in his office."

Drawings are required to accompany an application for trade-mark. The form and execution of the drawings are governed by strict rules, and must show a facsimile of the mark. We attend to the preparation of the drawings when application is made through us

A trade-mark entitled to registration may constitute any nondescriptive word or words, symbol, picture, figure, sign, autograph, monogram, or a combination of any or all of these. It need not be new or original, but it must be new to the purpose to which it is to be applied. "Eureka Shoes" would not be an infringement on "Eureka Tobacco."

A descriptive word cannot be registered, that is, a word which denotes the composition, quality, or attributes of goods can not be exclusively appropriated. Thus "Fine Cut," as applied to tobacco, could not be registered, because it is descriptive, and any one making fine-cut tobacco is entitled to so describe the same.

A geographical word, denoting origin of the goods, can not be registered. For example, no one could acquire the exclusive right to the word "Minnesota" for flour. All residents of Minnesota have that privilege.

A mere name of a person cannot be registered, because, generally speaking, every person has a right to the use of his own name on goods manufactured by him. But his autograph is distinctive and individual, and can be registered as a trade-mark.

Persons intending to adopt a trade-mark are advised to adopt some arbitrary or fanciful word or sign, meaningless as applied to the article. Thus "Dove," as applied to hams, is a good trade-mark, as it is entirely arbitrary and meaningless.

Medical compounds are usually protected by trade-marks of late years, it being practically impossible to secure a patent on this class of compounds. Indeed a trade-mark affords the better protection for compounds, compositions and preparations in many instances, as the ingredients and proportions or method of preparation need not be revealed to obtain the trade-mark registration.

Foreign registration of trade-marks may be secured in all countries with which the United States has treaties.

We will advise, free of charge, whether any particular trade-mark is a proper subject for registration.

Trade-marks heretofore registered under the old law should be again registered under the new act, because of additional rights and remedies provided by the new law and applicable only to trade-marks registered thereunder after March 31, 1905. The protection extends to interstate commerce, instead of foreign commerce as heretofore, and the rights are so enlarged and means for enforcing the trade-mark so improved that the small expenditure required is fully warranted

LABELS AND PRINTS.

A label is "an artistic representation or intellectual production impressed or stamped directly upon articles of manufacture, or upon any slip or piece of paper or other material, to be attached in any manner to manufactured articles, or to bottles, boxes, and packages containing them, to indicate the contents of the package, the name of the manufacturer, or the place of manufacture, the quality of goods, directions for use, etc." (Patent Office Rule.)

A print is "an artistic representation or intellectual production not borne by the article of manufacture or vendable commodity, but in some fashion pertaining thereto—such, for instance, as an advertisement thereof." (Patent Office Rule.)

Labels and prints, to be entitled to registration, must be artistic in nature or design, and not mere typesetters' skill. Fancy labels used on cigar boxes, and pictures or posters used in advertising, are examples of registrable labels and prints. Such labels and prints are registrable in the Patent Office under the act of June 18, 1874,—the Copyright Law.

COPYRIGHTS.

A copyright may be secured by the author, designer, or proprietor of any book, map, chart, dramatic or musical composition, engraving, cut, print or photograph or negative thereof, painting, drawing, chromo, statuary, model or design, as a work of fine art.

Following is a list of articles which are **not** subject to copyright registration:

Account books,
Advertising devices and novelties,
Albums,
Articles of manufacture,
Badges, buttons and medals,
Blank agreements,
Blank books,
Blank cards,
Blank forms,
Book covers,
Bonds,
Borders,
Business names,
Cards (playing),
Cards (score),
Catchwords,
Coined words or names,
Coupons, or coupons systems,
Emblems,
"Endless chains,"
Engravings of manufactured articles,
Fancy articles,
Fans,
Flags,
Form of words,
Games and puzzles, (although the instructions for playing the same may be),
Letter heads,

Manufactured articles,
Mechanical devices,
Medicines,
Memorandum books,
Mere names, words, or phrases,
Note headings,
Ophthalmic test cards,
Pads,
Paper hangings,
Paper weights,
Pass books,
Patterns,
Pedigree blanks,
Scrap books,
Signs,
Stamps,
Stickers,
Systems,
Tickets of any kind,
Time books,
Trade-marks,
Words (coined),
Words or phrases,
Wrappers for articles to be sold.

Copyrights are assignable by an instrument of writing, and must be recorded within 60 days after execution "in default of which it shall be void as against any subsequent purchaser or mortagee for a valuable consideration, without notice." (Rev. Stat., Sec. 4955.)

The period of protection by copyright is 28 years, renewable for 14 more.

MILO B. STEVENS & CO.,
Attorneys.

Established 1864.

OFFICES:
817 14th St. N. W., Washington, D. C.
163 Randolph St., Chicago, Ill.
231 The Arcade, Cleveland, O.
401 Whitney Bldg., Detroit, Mich.

Form of fee contract required in cases undertaken on the contingent plan. (See page 7.)

INSTRUCTIONS.—The following contract for the contingent payment of our fee should be signed by you, with one witness to your signature, and deposited in bank with the specified amount to our order, **and have the bank notify us that the contract has been deposited without alteration, together with the stipulated amount which will be held in the bank until the fee is payable.** If you cannot conveniently do this have the contract guaranteed by some other responsible person, who is known at some bank, and send it to us.

FEE CONTRACT

of ....
with MILO B. STEVENS & CO., ATTORNEYS, OF WASHINGTON, CHICAGO, CLEVELAND AND DETROIT.

BE IT KNOWN, That, in consideration of services rendered and to be rendered by MILO B. STEVENS & CO., of ....
....
as attorneys in the preparation and prosecution of my application for
....
on ....
at the U. S. Patent Office.

I HEREBY CONTRACT AND AGREE to pay said MILO B. STEVENS & CO., a fee of $................... upon receipt of notice of allowance of my said application: *Provided, however*, That if their power of attorney be revoked by me or my assigns before the allowance of the application, then the above stipulated fee shall become immediately payable to said STEVENS & CO., without reference to the official status of the application. *And provided further*, That it is understood that the above stipulated fee has reference only to the ordinary course of prosecution, and does not relate to extraordinary proceedings, such as appeals or interference contests, if any become necessary.

WITNESS MY HAND this ....day of..........., 190..

....
Witness sign here.   Inventor sign here.
                                ....

GUARANTY.

I hereby guarantee the payment of the above stipulated fee.
        (Name)..
        (Business)...
        (Address)...
Dated ...., 190..

TESTIMONIALS.

We print below a few of the many testimonials we have received from satisfied clients:

From H. H. Bonney, Fairmount, Minn.: "Your promptness, business-like actions and honesty through the whole transaction was very satisfactory and I would recommend those seeking to secure patents to employ you, as I shall do when I have more work of this kind."

From George W. Brown, Jamestown, N. Y.: "You certainly handled my patent business in a very able manner and with dispatch. Anything I may have in the future in your line you shall attend to."

From H. P. Coile, M. D., Knoxville, Tenn.: "I have received notice from the Patent Office of the allowance of my application for patent on Improvement in Bath Tubs and am very much pleased with the result. I take pleasure in expressing to you my appreciation of the manner in which you have handled my interest in the case."

From J. A. Dale, Dalesville, Pa : "It affords me great pleasure to say that your promptness in securing for me the United States and Canadian patents on my Improved Table Attachment for Chairs has been very satisfactory, and I commend your very thorough and efficient manner of conducting the patent business."

From Wm. B. Estes, Danville, Ill.: "For promptness and efficiency I highly recommend Milo B. Stevens & Co. to all inventors wanting quick and profitable results. This is my experience with these gentlemen."

From C. T. Mason, Sumter S. C.: "It is with much pleasure that I can testify to the very satisfactory service rendered me by your company in the preparation and prosecution of my patent case."

From Carl R. Culley, Norwalk, Ohio: "I am very much pleased with the manner and promptness with which you secured my patents. I shall place all future business in your hands"

From Samuel R Ford, Mt. Sterling, Ind.: "I have found you very thorough, persistent and faithful in the prosecution of my case before the Patent Office and I unhesitatingly recommend you to all inventors."

From McGaughey & Sheerer, Smith's Ferry, Pa · "We desire to thank you for your energy and dispatch in securing our patent and would recommend you to any one seeking like service "

From Knudt N. Knudtson, Beaver Creek, Minn.: "Your services in securing my patent on Music Leaf Turner gave me entire satisfaction as did also other business which you have done for me. I thank you for your promptness."

From James H. Tann, Dayton, Ohio· "I thank you for the able manner in which you have prosecuted by patent case and the success which has attended your efforts in my behalf. I can and will gladly recommend you to those in need of your services."

From C. R. Brock, Perry, Kans.: "I am well pleased with your work in the prosecution of my patent case."

From Jason D. Timmerman, Stone Mils, N. Y.: "It has been a pleasure to do business with you. You have been prompt, thorough and very faithful in the prosecution of my case, and I unhesitatingly recommend you to all inventors desiring good work."

From Coleman H. Wayman, Princeton, Mo.: "I was well pleased with your work in the prosecution of my patent case and shall have more business for you in the future."

From C. S. Hillabrandt, Gloversville, N. Y.: "Your prompt and good work has been very satisfactory and I would recommend you to any person desiring to take out a patent or trade-mark."

From J. H. Harris, Willow, Ark.: "Your prosecution of my patent case was entirely satisfactory."

From Henry Mahler, Pender, Neb.: "I am well pleased with the first-class work you performed in securing my patent on Sulky Plow."

From Jacob Vogt, Newburg, N. Y.: "I beg to acknowledge receipt of U. S. patent on Block Clamp and thank you for your careful attention to my case. Should I have any more to take out will call on you again."

From John M. Peitz, Elwood, Ind.: "I have marked your professional advance with interest and commend you as capable and efficient attorneys in patent cases."

From C. B. Robertson, Ottumwa, Iowa: "I am desirous of acknowledging my appreciation of the services you have rendered me in securing my patents and trust that I may be favored with your usual promptness and attention in future transactions."

From Levi Scarbrough, Centralia, Ill.: "I am well pleased with your work in securing my patent and am a thousand times obliged to you."

From Theo. A. Sease, Milan, Kans "Am perfectly satisfied in every respect with your work and can cheerfully recommend you as honest and trustworthy."

From C K. Tuggle, Columbus, Ohio. "I find the patent you secured for me beyond my expectations and thank you for your prompt action. I assure you my work in the future."

From John D. Witcher, Union Point, Ga.: "Am very much pleased with the result of your work in securing a patent on my Square, No. 734290. I highly recommend you to inventors."

From Fred S. Martin, Sioux City, Iowa: "I am very well satisfied with your services in my patent case."

From C. L. Robbins, Pekin, Ill.: "I am in receipt of letters patent in U. S. and Canada and wish to thank you for your kindness and the gentlemanly course which you pursued in prosecuting my case. Your services have been perfectly satisfactory in every way. I expect to apply for another patent through your firm very soon."

From John W. Hoskins, Clinton, Tenn.: "I hereby certify that Milo B. Stevens & Co. obtained a patent for me in less than four weeks and I can honestly recommend them to all who anticipate securing a patent and their clients have no need to be afraid of delays or overcharge."

From Richard Hunt, Mannington, Ky.: "I most heartily thank you for the loyalty and promptness which you exercised in securing my patent on Improved R. R. Tie. I can truly recommend your most faithful assistance."

From H. E. Kreuter, Nickel Plate, Ind.: "I am certainly highly pleased with the time in which you succeeded in getting my patent and will not fail to recommend you to every one who mentions patent."

From Andrew S. Lanum, Conneaut, Ohio. "I am well pleased with the way you transacted business for me, and would be glad to recommend you to anyone wanting their business attended to in a prompt and business-like manner."

From J. H. McConnell, Pulteney, N. Y.: "The patent on my invention on Combined Cane and Stool came very promptly to hand. I am well satisfied with your work and the prompt way in which you attended to my business."

From William Lee, Elwood, Ind.: "I am under many obligations for the prompt and honest service I received at your hands in the matter of securing my patent and of the broadest possible claims on my invention. I cheerfully recommend you to the public"

From Wm A. Mercer, Walnut, Ill. "Am well pleased with work done for my patent No. 731589."

From Wm. B. Michel, Versailles, Mo : "Your work in securing my patent on Improved Railway Track Layer far exceeded my expectations and am more than pleased with the same. I have more work in view for your firm in the near future."

From Wilson E. Moyer, Richland, Pa.: "Your work in securing a patent for me was entirely satisfactory, and I cheerfully recommend your services to all interested parties."

From Horace E. Nichols, Whitesboro, N. Y.: "In regard to securing patents I will say that Milo B. Stevens & Co. have been very prompt with me and have given me entire satisfaction with their work."

From T. Massey Short, New Lewisville, Ark.: "Your work in handling my patent on Cotton Chopper was more than satisfactory, and I can cheerfully recommend you to anyone desiring work in this line. Am working on another machine and expect to give you the handling of the case."

From Saxton C. Shoup, Fostoria, Ohio: "It affords me pleasure to say that your promptness in securing patent on my Preserving Compound has been very satisfactory and I commend your very thorough and efficient manner of conducting the patent business."

From A. Walter, Gorham, N. Y.: "The writer wishes to thank you for the dispatch and manner of securing patent and would be pleased to recommend your company to parties wishing to secure a patent."

From W. H. Williams, Slateford, Pa.: "It gives me pleasure to state that my transactions with you have been very satisfactory and I do not hesitate to recommend any one in need of a good Patent Solicitor to secure your services. Any future business in your line which I may have will be placed in your hands."

From E. H. Bonebrake, Roadside, Pa.: "I regard you as very thorough in the preparation of patent cases and unusually successful in securing what you claim."

From C. C. & C. S. Nichols, Roseland, Neb.: "We obtained a patent on Traction Wheel through Milo B. Stevens & Co. and do not hesitate to recommend them as reliable, energetic attorneys."

From John B. Cary, Peruque, Mo.: "I cheerfully recommend Milo B Stevens & Co. to any one wishing to secure a patent."

From George R. Jackson, McLean, Ill : "I have employed three different patent attorneys and can testify that you have done by far the best work for me."

From J. C. Blott, Waukesha, Wis.: "The patent you obtained for me on my Tacking Tool was first-class and I thank you for the good work done for me. I will recommend you to my friends in need of such service."

From Winfield Scott Barager, Hunt, N. Y.: "My patent, No. 734154, issued eighty days after filing application, has been received. Please accept my thanks for your kindness and the gentlemanly course which you pursued in my case. Your services have been perfectly satisfactory in every way."

From Charles A. Overton, Dunlap, Iowa: "I received my patent on Stove Pipe sooner than I expected and am perfectly satisfied with the way you prosecuted my case I hope to do further business with you."

From August F. Hein, Postville, Iowa: "I wish to express my appreciation of your courtesy and the speed with which you secured my patent. I shall show my satisfaction by giving you any further work I may have in your line."

From Joseph Herb, West Superior, Wis.: "I am perfectly satisfied with your work in securing the allowance of my trade-mark case."

From J. A. Peck, Springfield, Mo.: "The patent on Wagon which you secured for me was all I could ask. I also have another invention which I shall want patented "

From Josiah Pence, Nicholasville, Ky.: "Allow me to thank you for procuring for me the patent on my Seed Gatherer. I am especially well pleased with the prompt, fair and able way in which you managed the case and shall take pleasure in recommending your firm."

From Joseph Bertrand, Chicago, Ill.: "Please accept my thanks for your promptness in ascertaining the patentability of my invention. I will cheerfully recommend you to others."

From M. T. Bransfield, Chicago, Ill.: "The highly efficient manner in which my application for patent was prosecuted by your firm, together with the courteous treatment received at your hands at all times, have merited my utmost satisfaction and gratitude."

From John F. Doyle, Chicago, Ill. "Having had considerable professional work done by Milo B. Stevens & Co. and found that firm thoroughly honorable, conscientious and competent, I cheerfully recommend them to all prospective applicants for patents."

From John Hueni, Chicago, Ill.: "It gives me great pleasure to testify that the services of Milo B. Stevens & Co. in securing my patent were very satisfactory and any one desiring their services will make no mistake in employing them"

From Albert B. Gardella, Cleveland, Ohio: "I am more than pleased and satisfied with your work and will recommend you to any one having anything in your line."

From Andrew Juif, Detroit, Mich.: "I am especially pleased with your services in securing patents."

From John W. Pax, Chicago, Ill.: "As one of your clients I desire to inform you that your services in securing my patent have given entire satisfaction. Some future day I may call upon you again."

From Chas. C. Reid, Cleveland, Ohio: "I wish to thank you for your promptness in securing my patent as well as for your valuable advice, courteous treatment and business-like methods."

From C. H. Schenck, Cleveland, Ohio: "I wish to thank you for your promptness in securing my patent. I will recommend you to persons requiring the services of a reliable attorney."

From C. A. Sundgren, Chicago, Ill.: "I wish to express my satisfaction with your services in securing my patent. I am very much pleased with the results and shall call on you again when I need your services."

From Ira C. Stump, Cleveland, Ohio: "You may write anything to suit you over my signature by way of a good testimonial. I am anxiously looking for action on my present pending claim."

From E. Stevens and Chr. Terborg, Chicago, Ill.: "We are fully satisfied with your work in securing us a patent on Railway Gate. You were always ready to give advice and explanation."

From Wight & Hyatt, Cleveland, Ohio: "Our patent on Steam Boiler Furnace which you procured for us is just received. We beg to offer our thanks for the courtesy, patience, painstaking care and ability to grasp the details which you have uniformly shown in prosecuting this case We are pleased with the clearness of the specifications, and with the accuracy of the drawings, and believe you have served our best interests in the claims, and used all the points to the best advantage. We are very glad indeed to acknowledge our appreciation of your services."

From L. A. Wiseman, Cleveland, Ohio: "I am well pleased with your work in securing patent on my Combined Level and Square and if I ever have another case I will certainly let you handle it."

Following is a list of some of the persons for whom we have obtained patents:

Abbey, Wilson H., and Jacob Altmos, Ohio, Electrode.
Adams, Abram L., Ohio, Engine Drum Attachment.
Adams, William C., Iowa, Milk-pail Support.
Aldrich, Reginald D., Ill., Sprinkler Attachment.
Allen, Augustus V., Mo., Grooving Machine.
Allen, Leroy B., Ohio, Saddle.
Allen, Leroy B., Ohio, Checkrein Holder.
Anderson, Gotmar, N. D., Veterinary Forceps.
Applegate, Abra., Iowa, Stacker-Blower Governor.
Arnold, Phineas A., Ohio, Screening and Separating Apparatus.
Arnold, Robert, Ohio, Truss.
Ashby, Wm. H., Texas, Vehicle Tongue Support.
Astle, Richard T., Wyo., Cooking Utensil.
Avery, Mary L., Cal., Dress-chart.
Bailey, George D., Mich., Display Stand.
Baldwin, William I., and Everett A. Kline, Ohio, Paper-bag Machine.
*Baldwin, George A., Mo., Sound-conducting Horn.
Barager, Winfield S., N. Y., Washing Machine.
Barz, Paul H., Ill., Polishing Machine.
Baxter, George F., La., Saw-mill Carriage.
Bayard, Hyram J., Ill., Toy Bow.
Baylis, Chas. N., W. Va., Railway Switch.
Beardsley, Chauncey H., Ohio, Soft Tread Horseshoe.
Beeler, Esten B., Ill., Window Cleaner.
Bening, Edward W., Ill., Smoke-bell.
Bennett, Bruce, and John E. Moore, Ill., Clod Crusher.
Berman, John, Ill., Binder.
Berry, David C., Pa., Cross-head.
Berry, Matthew S., Me., Rowlock.
Bertrand, Joseph, Ill., Saw Level.
Blake, Fred W., Ohio, Furnace.
Blanchard, Thos. E., Colo., Design.
Blee, Chas. O., and James H. Redding, Fence-post.
Blot, John C., Wis., Tacking Tool.
Blum, Joseph, Ill., Towel-holder.
Blum, Joseph, Ill., Sink Attachment.

Bonney, Henry H., Minn., Mop-cabinet.
Bordner, William R., Ohio, Fence-post.
Bonebrake, Edw. H., Pa., Cultivator.
Bosemer, Charles, Ill., Oven.
Bostwick, Charles I., Minn., Grain Wagon or Tank Lining.
Bowers, John C., and Edward Dool, Ill., Egg-tester.
Bowers, John H., La., Pruning Implement.
Bowling, Fred'k T., Md, Damper and Spark Arrester.
Bransfield, Michael T., Ill., Horse Stock.
Brock, Clarence R., and William C. Barth, Kans., Fan.
Broderick, Robt., and Frank W. Gordon, Ohio, Electric-arc Lamp.
Brousseau, Harry, Wis., Hatch.
Brown, Francelia, N. Y., Game Apparatus.
Brown, George W., Ohio, Process.
Brown, Jacob W., Mass., Game-board Design.
Brown, Robt. E., Va., Well-borer.
Brown, Wm. H., Ohio, Concrete Machine.
Buckley, Chas., and Isaac C. Hollinger, Ind., Check-hook.
Bunce, Earl M. (2), Ohio, Rail-tie.
Burgin, Welby W., Ky., Dental Engine Attachment.
Butcher, Elmer E, Ohio, Wireless Telegraphy.
Byrne, Michael F., Iowa, Door.
Carlson, Axel, Ill., Rein Holder.
Carpenter, John H. and Chas., Ill., Massage Instrument.
Carrick, Wm. B., Ill., Gas-burner.
Carter, James H., Ill., Cell Case.
Cary, John B, Ill., Wagon Brake.
Chapman, Geo. E., Geo. L. Ensign and John M. Weir, Ohio, Trolley-wheel.
Chapman & Ensign, Ohio, Trolley.
Chapman, Frank J., Pa., Pneumatic Hammer Casing.
Chapman, George E., Ohio, Trolley-wheel Bearing.
Chartrand, Edmund, Ill., Scaffold
Cherer, Merrell A., Texas, Scaffold.
Chilcote, Maurice A, Ohio, Belt Fastener.
Christinsen, Anton, Ill, Car-brake.
Christy, James, Jr., D. C., Tire.
Clarke, John S., Mich., Flue-cleaner.
Clark, John and Albert Holft, Ill., Gas-burner.
Coffey, Michael, Ill., Garment Clasp
Compton, Chas. H., Ill., Lamp-burner.
Cook, Irving A., Ohio, Sewing-machine Horn.
Cooper, George B. F., Mich, Brake-beam Fulcrum.
Cooper, George B. F., Mich., Brake-beam and Attachment.

Culley, Carl R., Ohio, Numbering Machine.
Culley, Carl R., Ohio, Printing-press.
Curlett, Lewis K., Ill., Electrical Signal.
Cusick, Thomas, N. D., Car-coupling.
Daniels, Cyrus D., Ohio, Book Support.
Darling, Edward J., Pa., Combination Article.
Deckand, Thomas E., Ohio, Printing-frame Holder.
Deppe, Nelson R. (2), N. C., Lumber-jack.
Dickson, Geo. F., and Ellsworth E. Bower, Ill., Clenching Tool.
Dill, Edward S., Ill., Door Hanger.
Ditty & Ordner, Ohio, Trade-mark.
Dahoney, Priscilla W., Ky., Lifter and Conveyer.
Dorffel, Chas., Ill., Holding-plate Design.
Doty, Alphonso H., Minn., Match-box Holder.
Douglas, Benj. B., Mo., Holder.
Dunham, Wm. J., N. Y., Leather-working Machinery.
Durand, John, Ga., Printing-press.
Durand, John, Ga., Hand-stamp.
Edsen, Alfred C., Ill., Coin-controlled Apparatus.
Einfalt, John A., Neb., Sliding-door Hanger.
Eldredge, Mary E., Pa., Toy Furniture.
Embry, John R., Kans., Wind-motor.
Emery, Ned H., Iowa, Hay-rack.
Esser, Lawrence, Mo., Nut-lock.
Estes, William B., Ill., Furnace.
Evered, Herbert C. (Ill.) and John F. (Mo.), Clothes-drier.
Field, Jacob W., Ill., Cigar-cutter.
Fiveash, Zion E., Mo., Rail Joint.
Flanagin, Herschel H., Mich., Store Cabinet.
Ford, Samuel R., Ind., Sleigh Runner.
Fortier, Edmond, Ill., H. P. Indicator.
Foster, William S., Ill., Cutting-machine.
French, Richmon E., Ohio, Bottle Design.
Gaines, Thomas K., Texas, Artificial Stone.
Galbraith, Wm. T., Alexander Weaver and James W. Sconce, Mo., Steam-boiler.
Gale, Henry, Ill., Hoof Protector.
Galey, John M., Texas, Cylinder-cock.
Gantt, William M. and James M., S. C., Wagon-brake.
Garvey, Francis J., Ill., Pail.
Gelabert, William P., and Thos. G. Nelson, Mo., Buckle Design.
Geisel, Mary, W. Va., Folding Bed.
Gilling, Chas J., Ill., Tire.
Golden, Arville A., and Emma L., Ohio, Nut-lock.

Grindell, Chas. S., Ohio, Whiffletree-hook.
Groom, Isaac E., Kans, Mowing-machine.
Groomes, Asal, Mich., Telescope.
Guyot, Mary, Ill., Chair.
Hamilton, Edward D., Wash., Washing Machine.
Hamilton, Henry A., Pa., Brush Design.
Hamilton, John F., Ind., Exhaust-nozzle.
Hansen, Christian, Ill., Hand Stamp.
Harmon, John, Ill., Conveyer
Harpold, Christopher, Cal., Fruit-cutter.
Harris, John, Ohio, Gas-burner.
Hatfield, Guy M., O. T., Clothes-pin Design.
Hawkinson, Chas. H., Ill., Burglar Alarm and Door Check.
Hawkinson, Chas. H., Ill., Sash Lift and Lock.
Hazard, Clark D., Ohio, Heating-furnace.
Heberling, Albert T, Pa., Trade-mark.
Heizer, John W., Ill., Electric Fixture Support.
Hemphill, Martin L, Ind., Horse Stock.
Henry, Thomas J., Iowa, Scraper.
Hepburn, Martin E, Ill., Switch.
Hepp, Daniel, Ill., Time Recorder.
Herb, Joseph, Wis., Trade-mark.
Herbst, Frederick, Colo., Miner's Tool.
Hildebrand, Albert, Iowa, Tender.
Hill, Robert S., Mich, Conveyer.
Hillabrant, Clement S., N. Y., Trade-mark.
Hine, Thomas W., Iowa, Nut-lock.
Hoffman, Louis E., Ohio, Air-pump.
Hoffman, Louis E., Ohio, Boiler Feeder.
Holmgren, Oscar F., Ill., Composing-stick.
Holten, James McK., N. J., Oyster-tongs.
Hughes, William W., Ohio, Bicycle-saddle Cover.
Hurst, Eugene D., Neb., Threshing Machine.
Ingersoll, John L., Mich., Potato-digger.
Inskeep Edmund A., Ill, Nose Guard
Israelson, Iver C., S. D, Vise Attachment.
Jackson, George R., Ind., Saw.
James, John T., O T., Cotton-chopper.
Jenske, Gus A, Chas. A. Homrig and Eugene M. Blaine, Ill., Hook.
Johnson, Robert S, Mich, Crate.
Johnson, William T., Texas, Bale-tie.
Jones, Herbert D, Ill., Bottle-cap.
Jones, Thomas B, Ky, Screen.
Joubert, Joseph, Ill., Bracket.

Juif, Andrew, Mich., Cooling and filling apparatus.
Kelly, John A., and Steph. W. Rouse, Minn., Mill.
Kersey, Edward, Ill., Bottle.
Kesselring, Jacob, Mich., Cuspidor Design.
Kesselring, Philip, Jr., S. D., Fanning-mill.
Ketelsen, Andrew J., Ill., Separating-pan.
Kibbe, William A., Kans, Trestle.
Kildow & Lowry, Ohio, Trade-mark.
King, John H., Mich, Hay and Stock Rack.
King, Thos. W., Ohio, Damper.
Kinkade, Thos, Wyo., Rod-packing.
Klickman, Robt., Ill., Knife.
Klopsch, Osmar, N. Y., Trade-mark.
Knutson, Peter C., Wis., Corn-shocker.
Koeller, Wm. F., and Henry Dyer, Mich., Lathe-tool.
Koenig Chas L., Texas, Blind-stop.
Koryta, Chas., Ohio, Press-board.
Koze, Frank, Ohio, Hydraulic Motor.
Krant, Chas., Ill., Transfer Process.
Kughler, John H., Ill., Elevator Appliance.
Kuler, Leo., Pa., Wrench.
Lacey, Oliver C., Va., Fire-extinguishing Compound.
Lacey, Oliver C., Va., Fire-proofing Compound.
Latham, Geo. W., Mc., Boring-tool.
Lautenbach, Evert, Ill., Skirt-lifter.
Lautenbach, Evert, Ill., Rule.
Lavender, Thos. J., Mich., Chopping-knife.
Lawton, Henry B., Ill, Griddle.
Leach, Amos W., Ind, Safety Device.
Lepart, Warren W, Mich., Chair.
Levarm, Lewis H., Vt., Trap.
Levitin, Jakob, and Jacob Roser, Ill., Clothes-pounder **Design.**
Light, Frank, Colo, Flushing Apparatus.
Lilly, Francis G., Ohio, Potato-digger.
Lipps, William, Tenn., Water Elevator.
Loeb, George, Jr., Ohio, Washtub.
Magie, Wilbur R., Ohio, Feed-tank.
Mahler, Henry, Neb., Plow.
Mains, Wm. F. and Oliver E, Ohio, Truck.
Mallot, Hiram V., and Chas. K. Tuggle, Ohio, **Valve.**
Mangelsdorf, Edward C., Ill., Car.
Marsalis, Elijah, Miss., Plow Attachment.
Marshall, John W., Mont., Clamp.
Martin, Fred S., Neb., Gas-cock Lock.

Martin, Herman, Ohio, Wire-fence Machine.
Mason, Chas. T., S. C., Telephone-transmitter Joint.
Mathews, William, Ohio, Saw Set.
Mattoch, Robert L., Ill., Sheet Music Carrier.
McConnell, James H., N. Y., Combined Cane and Stool.
McChesley, Hugh M., Ohio, Horseshoe.
McChesley, Hugh M., Ohio, Nut-lock.
McFatridge, Charles M., Ohio, Wire Bender.
McGaughey, Samuel J., and Jacob Sheerer, Pa., Barrel.
McGeorge, Percy A. (2), N. Y., Conduit.
Mead, Edwin E., Ill., Car-seal.
Meams, Thos. V., Wash., Meat Needle and Larder.
Medford, Fred E., O. T., Computing Scale.
Melrose, Wm A., Ind., Crate Filler.
Mercer, William A., Ill., Music-leaf Turner.
Merritt, Willard M., Mich., Culinary Vessel.
Mills, Percy B., Mich., Mold.
Miller, Allen L., Ill., Tire.
Milner, Albert R, Ohio, Chair.
Mollitor, Joseph A, Ill., Bedstead.
Morris, John, Ark., Well-strainer.
Moss, Bertie B., Ind., Rail-tie.
Moss, Bertie B., Ind, Nut-lock.
Moss, Bertie B., Ind., Tie-plate.
Moyer, Wilson E., Pa., Can.
Myers, Benj. R., and Chas. A. Jacoby, Ill., Umbrella.
Myers, Jos. R., and Benj. R., Ill., Hat-tip.
Nelson, Chas. M., and John A. Christianson, Ill., Vessel.
Newman, Herman, Mich., Crib.
Nichols, Horace E., N. Y., Contact-post Design.
Nielsen, Peder, Mich,, Excavator.
Newdyke, William, Wis., Door.
Newport, Thos. L., Cal., Bath-brush.
Nichols, Claude and Chas. C., Neb., Wheel.
Niemeyer, Henry W., Ill., Handle.
Niggli, Emil (2), Texas, Cheese-cutter.
Nolan, John F., Ill., Molding-machine.
Norrington, Nova Z., Ind , Valve.
Norris William E., Mo., Clamp.
Odell, Levi J., Ill., Bread-cutting Machine.
O'Donnell, Mich. J., Ill., Motor Vehicle.
Olds, Fred P., Ohio, Shoe Last Design.
Orvis, Charles W., Mo., Vise.
Ogle, Chas. N., and Isaac K. Hurt, Ohio, Pulley.

Oines, Ole, S. D., Clothes-pounder.
O'Malley, Howard M., Ohio, Wheel.
Overton, Chas. A., Iowa, Stovepipe-joint.
Palser, George N., Tiberius McCall and Fred H. McCall, Neb., Clamp.
Parham, Horace M., S. C., Inking Roller.
Park, Alexander, and Chas. During, Ohio, Manufacture of Shovels.
Park, Andrew J., I. T., Switch Signal.
Parrett, Edgar E., Ind., Desk Attachment.
Patrick, Chas. H., Ill., Surgical Chair.
Pawley, Ernest C., and Wm. H. Miller, Ill., Tank and Heater.
Pax, John W., Ill., Holder Design.
Peacock, George J., Ind., Fan.
Peddy, Andr. J., Tenn., Chair.
Peek, James A., Mo., Hub-attaching Device.
Pence, Josiah, Ky., Seed-gatherer.
Penrod, John F., Pa., Rein-support.
Pertz, John W., Ind., Feed-water Heater and Purifier.
Phifer, John N., Ill., Electrical Generating-machine.
Phillips, John, Ill., Square.
Pond, Harry S., Ill., Cuff-holder.
Poole, Samuel E., Ohio, Explosive-engine Starter.
Porter, Sam'l A. S., S. C., Rotary-engine.
Post, Alva W., Kans., Wire-fence Tool.
Post, Claude L., Ill., Calendar.
Preston, James, Ill., Trolley-wheel.
Putnam, Joseph W., and Wm. Harman, Mich., Cabinet.
Quist, John, and Jas. A. Bain, Ohio, Gas-generator.
Ramsey, Deloss, Kans., Band-cutter and Feeder.
Randall, Lucius R., Ga., Combination Farming Machine.
Randall, Lucius, R., Ga., Shovel-plow.
Randall, Mercy J., Mo., Wardrobe and Dresser.
Ray, Albert D., Ohio, Fender Fastening.
Raymond, Chas M., and Louis E. Hoffman, Ohio, Steam-boiler.
Raymond, Chas. M., Ohio, Steam-boiler.
Reid, Chas. C., Ohio, Igniter.
Ress, Frank L., Ohio, Square and Bevel.
Reynolds, Frank M., Iowa, Cooler and Aerator.
Reznick, Oscar, Ill., Ironing Board.
Rider, Ebenezer W., Mich., Alarm.
Roark, Mortimer B., Texas, Violin-bow.
Robbins, Cordilleras L., Ill., Door.
Robertson, Chas. B. (2), Iowa, Trolley-catcher.
Robertson, Chas. B. and John J., Iowa, Insulator.
Rohwedder, Detlef H. (2), Ill., Propeller.

Root, William H., Ill., Scaffold.
Rosencrantz, Isador B., Ill., Tuning-pin Cover.
Rosencrantz, Isador B., Ill., Trade-mark.
Rumple, James T., Texas., Burner.
Ryan, Edward, and Johnson, Oscar, Iowa, **Tender.**
Ryer, Walter E., N. Y, Trolley-wheel.
Sabin, Herbert B., Ohio, Folding Support.
Sarbach, Fred, Ohio, Trolley-harp Design.
Say, Zoe B., Pa , Index.
Scarbrough, Levi, Ill., Fruit Gatherer.
Scharkofshy, Rudolph, Ohio, Tenpin.
Schell, James D., Ill., Bottle-capping Machine.
Schenck, Claud H. E., Ohio, Wheel Fender.
Schmoldt, Barney F., Walter, Frederick C., Ohio, **Wheel Fender.**
Schopf, Amos, Mo., Tile-laying Machine.
Schott, Hugo, Ill., Cornice-brake Machine.
Scott, Oliver P , Ill., Incubator.
Scott, Oliver P., Ill., Incubator Heater.
Sease, Theo. A., Kans., Shade Hanger.
Setbacken, Peter J., Ind., Gate-latch.
Settergren, Bernard, Ill., Vaporizer.
Shafer, Riley A., Ohio, Bit.
Shaw, Jesse T., Ill., Rail-tie.
Shaw, John, Pa., Reamer.
Sherrill, Francis M., Kans., Cultivator and **Weed Cutter.**
Short, Robert L., Ohio, Cannon.
Short, T. Massey, Ark., Cotton Chopper.
Shoup, Saxton C.. Ohio, Preserving Compound.
Shue, Philip H. (3), Colo., Concentrator.
Simmons, John C , Tenn., Fence.
Skinner, Burr R , Iowa, Lunch Box.
Sly, Wm W., Ohio, Barrel-closure.
Sly, Wm. W., Ohio, Dust-collector.
Smith, Wm. H., Kans., Rake and Marker.
Solar Prism Co , Ohio, Trade-mark.
Somers, Frank P., Ohio Automatic Cut-off.
Southworth, Preston B , Oregon, Hook.
Springard, Joseph, N J , Awning Support.
Squires, Henry G (2), Pa., Ink-well.
Stafford, Joseph Z , Mont., Plow.
Stevens, Egbert, and Terborg, Christian, Cal. and Ill., **Signal.**
Stewart, Wm. M., Colo., Stirrup.
Stichle, Samuel L. S., Cal., Door-check.
Stickler, Elias, Iowa, Gate.

Stoddard, Merritt L., Ohio, Washing Machine.
Stoll, Charles, Ill., Fire-escape.
Stoppel & Andrews, Ohio, Trade-mark.
Stow, Burt E., Mont., Roller.
Straight, Edward B., Ill., Music Rack.
Stump, Ira A., Ohio, Screwdriver.
Sundgren, Carl A., Ill., Shoe-brushing Machine.
Sutherland, Lucy A., Ill., Hook and Eye.
Sutton, Wm. D., Ohio, Whiffletree Hook.
Tams, James H., Mich., Musical Instrument.
Teele, John W., Texas, Spike.
Thomas, Benj. K., Nebr., Coupling.
Thompson, Chas., Ill., Bedstead.
Thompson, James G., Wyo., Sash Fastener.
Thompson & Simpson, Tenn., Trade-mark.
Thornton, James H., Ill., Sash Lock.
Timmerman, Jason D., N. Y., Lightning Protector.
Trosh, Reuben S., Mich., Moving Device.
Tulley, John W., Mo., Coin-controlled Box.
Tulley, John W., Mo., Case.
Turner, Chas. R., Mass., Truss.
Tverdahl, Ole., Ohio, Sad-iron.
Vachon, George C., Ill., Ornamenting Wood.
Vessely, Frank J., Ind., Hay Fork.
Vogt, Jacob, N. Y., Clamp.
Walter, Christian P., Ill., Caster.
Warner, Maggie, Ill., Strainer.
Washburn, George P., Nebr., Gas Purifier.
Washburn, George P. (2), Nebr., Acetylene Gas Generator.
Wayman, Coleman H., Mo., Cartridge Ejector.
Weidenbaker, Edmund, Ill., Flask.
Wells, Clinton, Colo., Windmill.
Westbrook, Troy D., Fla., Well-driving Hammer.
Weston, Oliver, Ohio, Tool-handle Wedge.
Whitney, Arthur E., Ill., Hot-air Feeder.
Wieburg, Frank L., Minn., Measuring Tank and Pump.
Williams, Nate, Mich., Combination Tool.
Williams, William H., Pa., Crane.
Wink, Chas., Ohio, Scow.
Wiszowaty, Adolph N., Ill., Trade-mark.
Witcher, John D., Ga., Square.
Wolfe, John W., Iowa, Ore Separator.
Woodley, Benj. R., Ill., Paint Pot.
Wooten, Augustus H., Ga., Combined Planter and Fertilizer Distributer.

Young, William H., and Hayer, Stephen A., Fla., Headlight.
Zaleski, Boleslaus, Ill., Trade-mark.
Zatzhe, Daniel, Ill., Window Frame.
Zilkie, John, Ill., Whistle.
Robbins, C. L., Ill., Grain-Car Door.
Rigg, J. C., Ky., Lifting-Jack.
Jas. L. Rhodes, Ark., Desk.
Reich, Otto F., Ill., Pillow.
Rafferty, Wm. J., Ill., Apparatus for Heating, Purifying, and Distributing Air in Buildings.
Rackle, Herman E., Ohio, Wall Construction.
Peterman, A. E., Ala., Telegraph Key.
Perry, Milo B., Ill., Soap-dispenser.
Pence, Josiah, Ky., Seed-gatherer.
Palmer, George W., Cal., Curtain-rod Support.
Page, R D., Mich., Automatic Crossing-gate
Olson, A. H., and Nyberg, C. E., Ill., Rotary Engine.
Morris, T. Eegar, Ill., Device for Opening and Closing Doors or Gates.
Miller, F. J., Ohio, Counterweight Attachment for Gas-engines.
Miller, Perry B., Mich., Mold.
M'chel, W. B., N. Y., Rail-joint.
McCain, F. W., West Va., Water-supply System
Maxson, F. E., Minn., Combined Water Still and Heater.
Lilly, F. G., Ohio, Potato-digger.
Erving, Andrew V., Mich., Stove.
Epes, T. P., Va., Tellurian.
Englert, Jos. J., Ill., Tag-wiring Machine.
Doyle, Jno F., Baseball-batting Apparatus.
DeGraff, H. W., N. Y., Wrench.
Dennis, Jno. J., Ill., Scaffold-bracket.
Fisher, H. J., Colo., Telephony.
Feehery, John Ill., Grain-separator.
Hegener, Rudolph, Ill., Wooden Column.
Hoover, O. C., Ohio, Soldering Compound.
Simmons, Elmer, Mo., Post-maul.
Sly, Wm. W., Ohio, Clutch.
Merkels, John B., Ill., Closure for Envelops or Bags.
Shufelt, Wm. R., N. Y., Vegetable-topping Machine.
Southwell, John A., Pa., Non-refillable Bottle.
Schiffer, P. J., Mich. Letter-box.